AF440495

TRACE LETTERS AND NUMBERS

Children's Reading & Writing Education Books

BABY PROFESSOR

EDUCATION KIDS

All Rights reserved. No part of this book may be reproduced or used in any way or form or by any means whether electronic or mechanical, this means that you cannot record or photocopy any material ideas or tips that are provided in this book

Copyright 2016

Practice writing letters and numbers

A is for Airplane

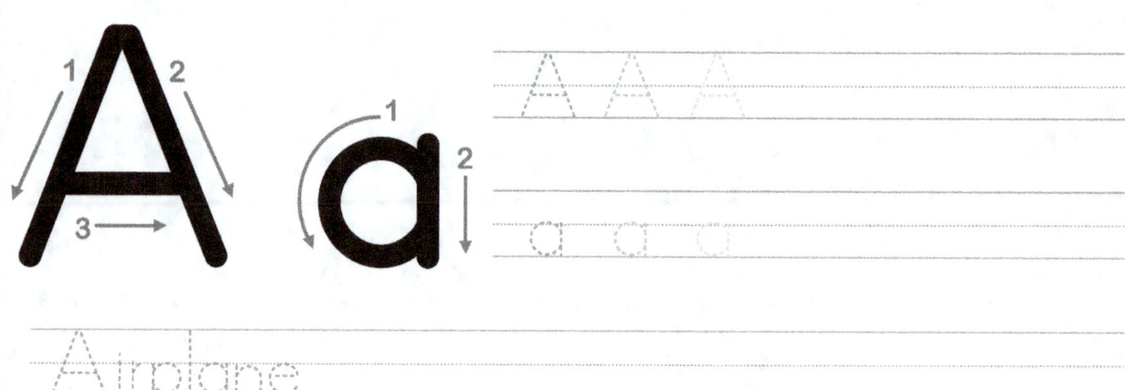

B is for Butterfly

C is for Cake

D is for **Donut**

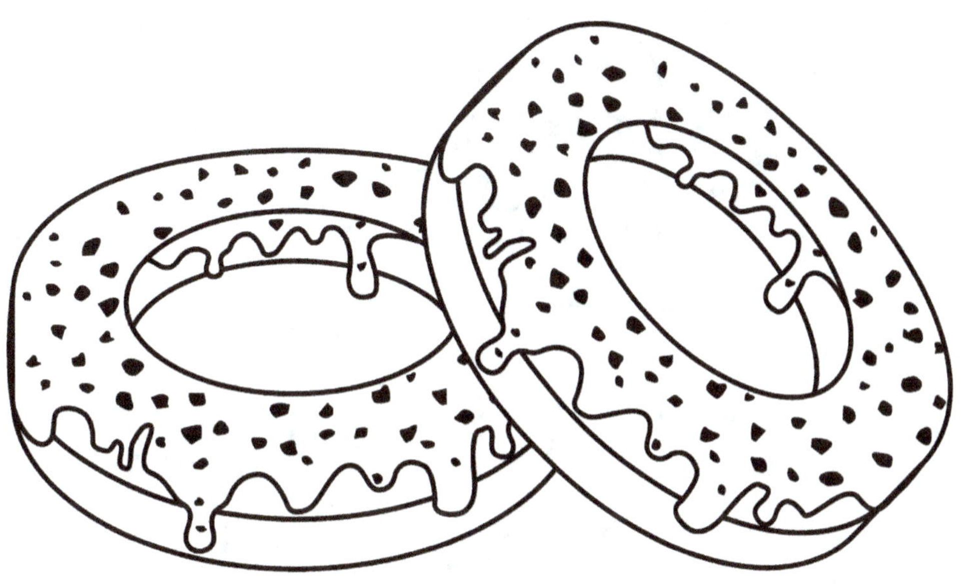

E is for **Eagle**

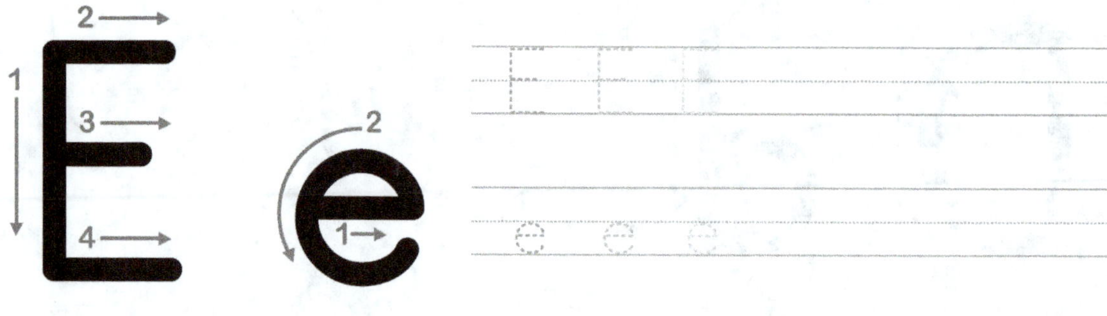

F is for **Fish**

G is for **Gumball**

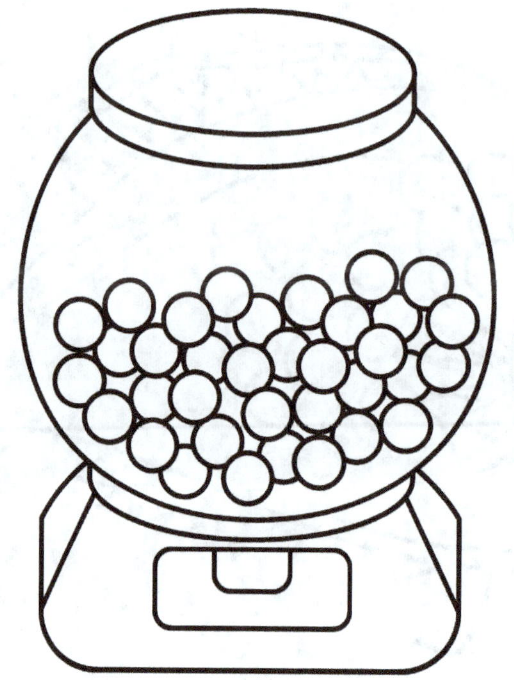

H is for House

I is for **Ice Cream**

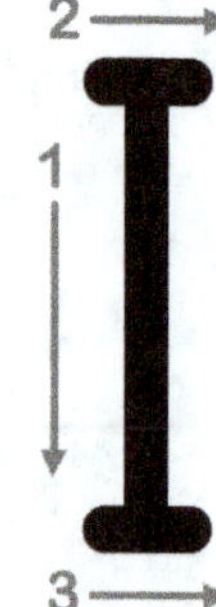

Ice Cream

J is for **Jam**

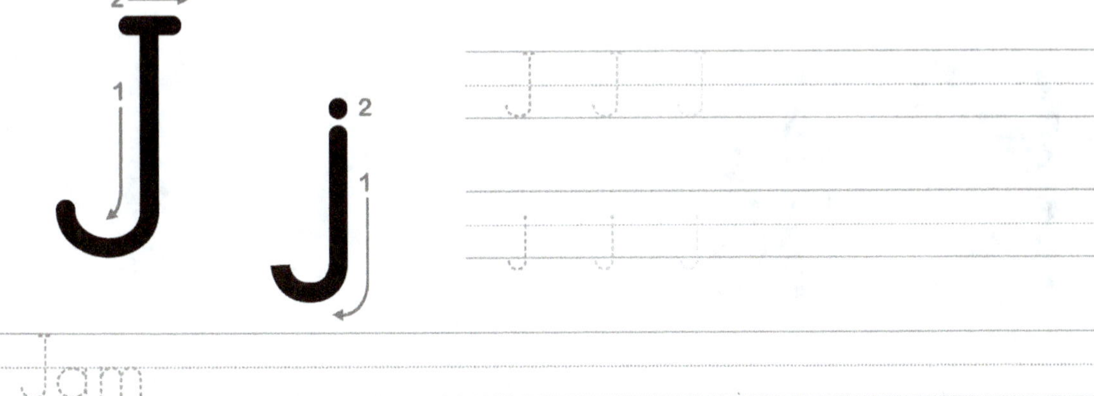

K is for **Koala**

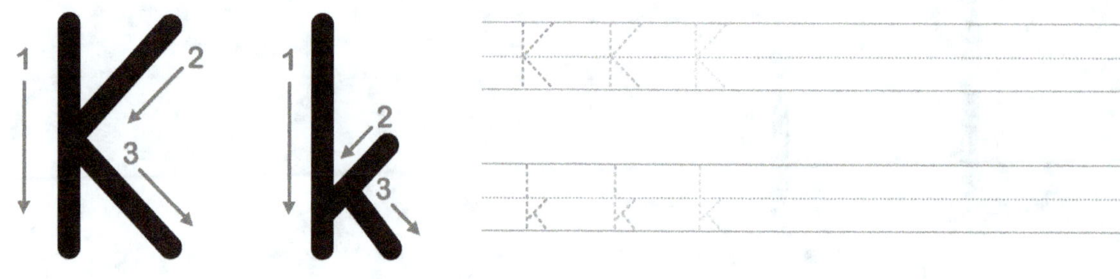

L is for **Ladybug**

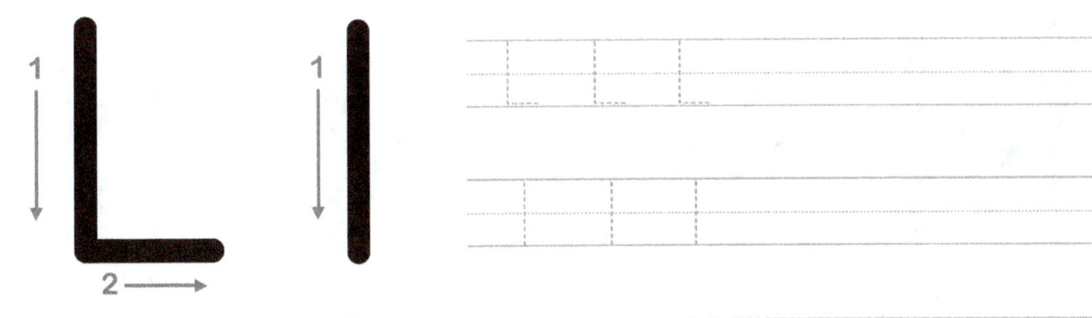

M is for Monkey

M m

Monkey

N is for **Nest**

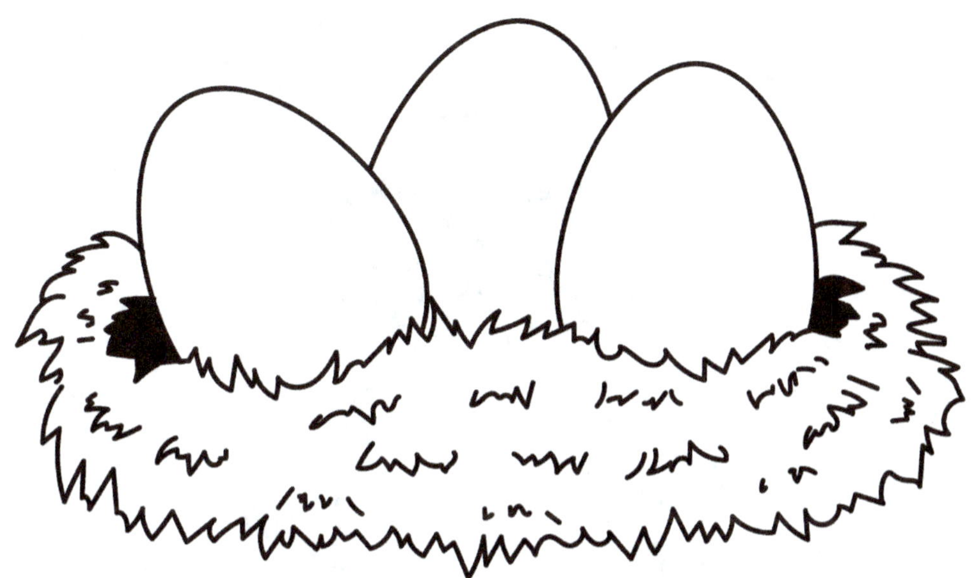

O is for Owl

P is for Penguin

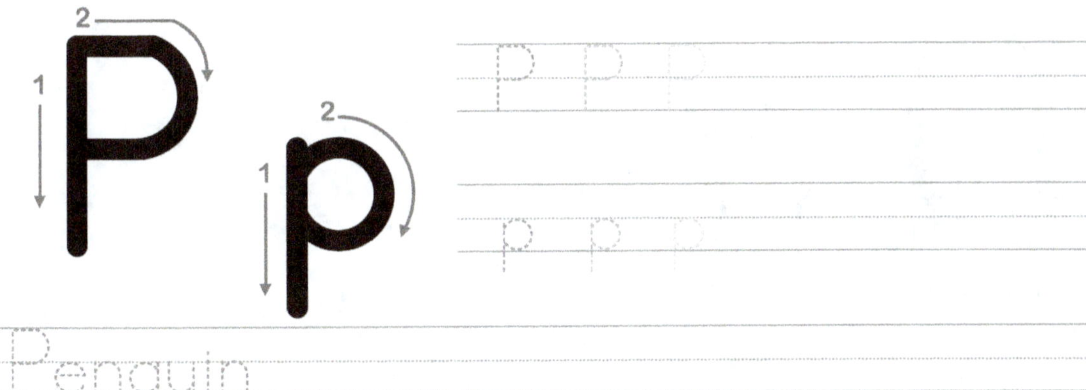

Q is for Queen

R is for Rainbow

S is for **Sun**

T is for **Tree**

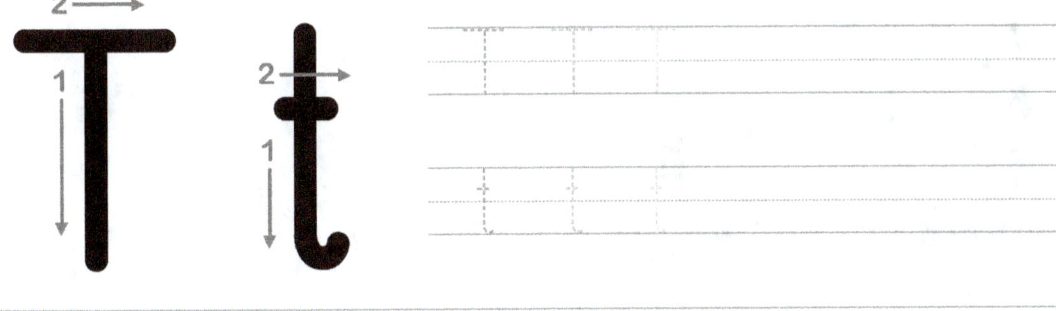

U is for **Umbrella**

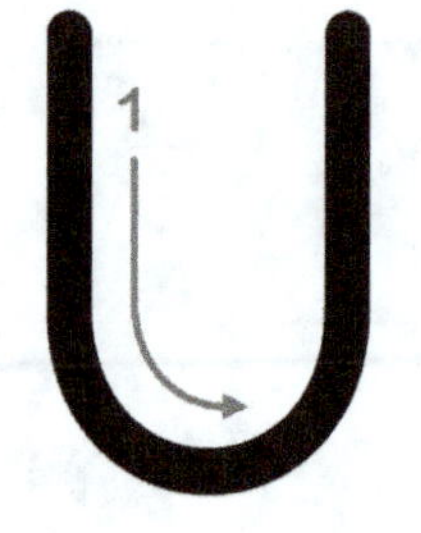

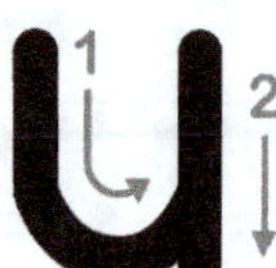

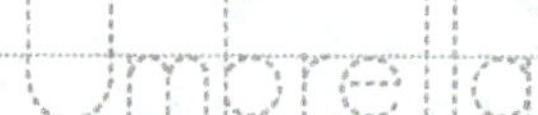

V is for **Vegetable**

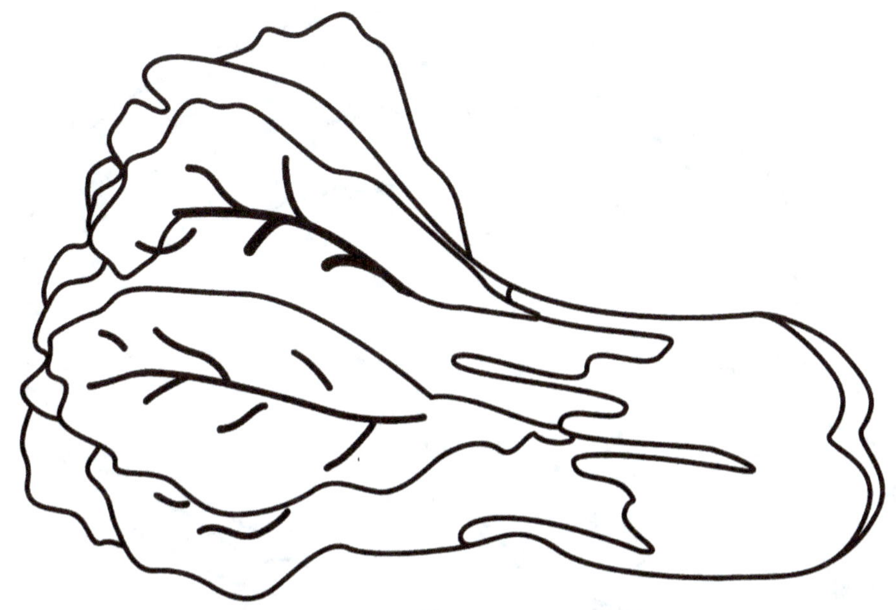

V v

Vegetable

W is for **Watermelon**

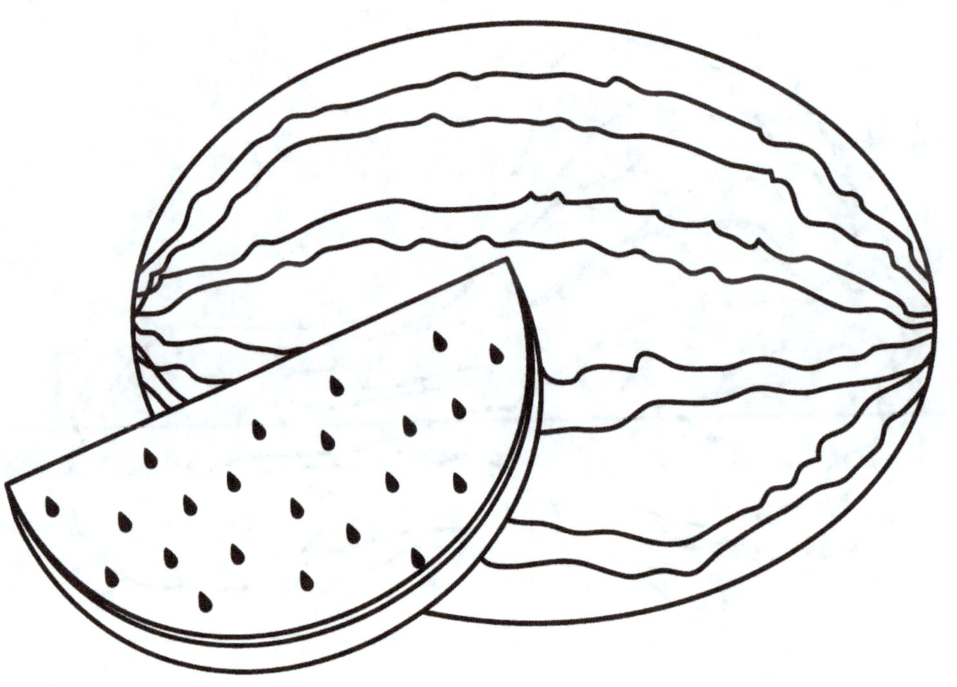

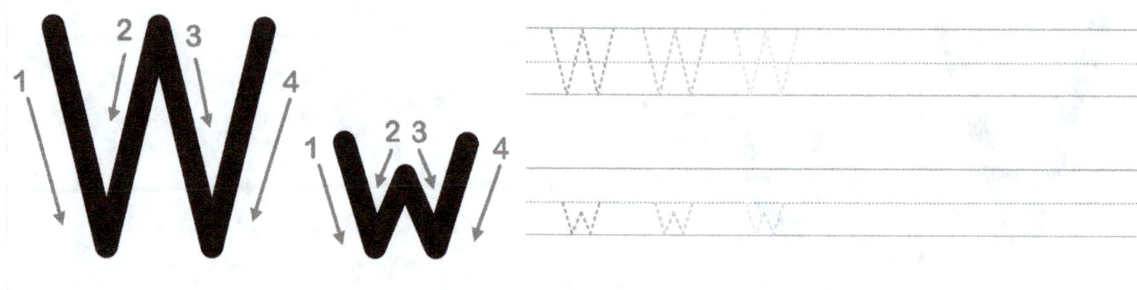

X is for **Xylophone**

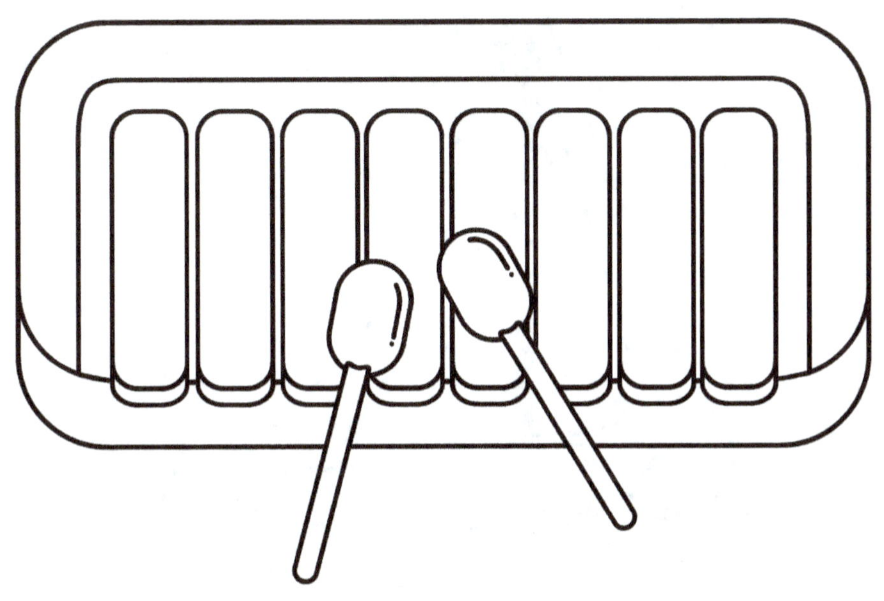

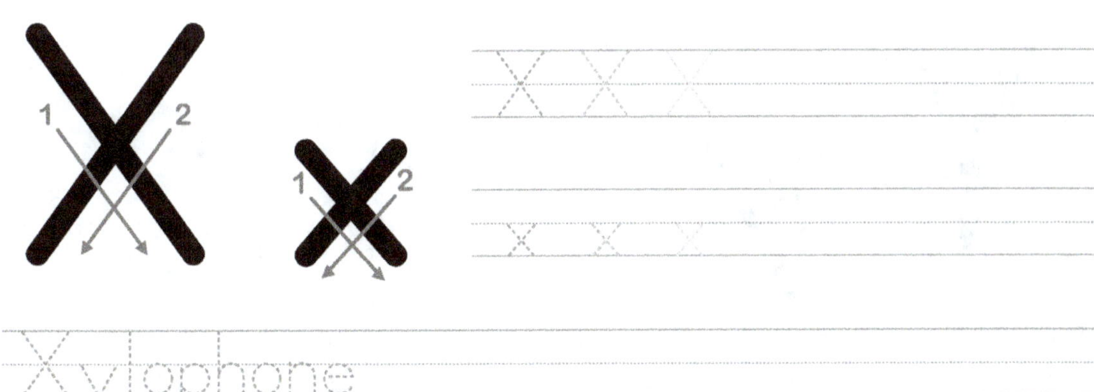

Y is for **Yacht**

Z is for **Zip**

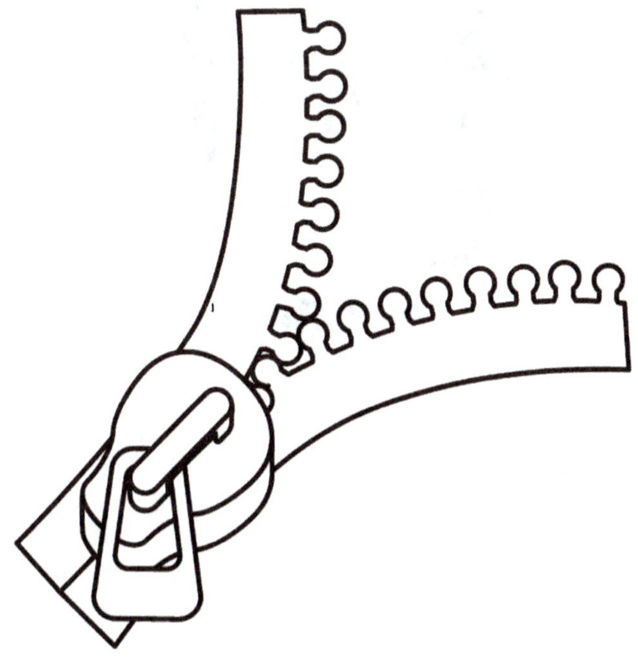

Z z

Zip

1
2
0 0 0 0 0 0
Zero Zero Zero

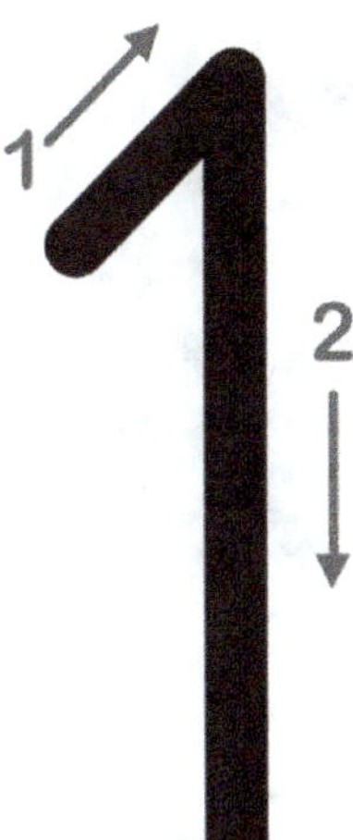
1
2

1 1 1 1
One One One

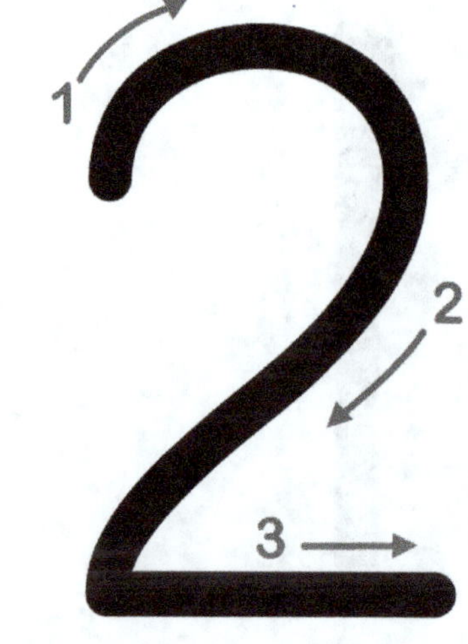

2 2 2 2
Two Two Two

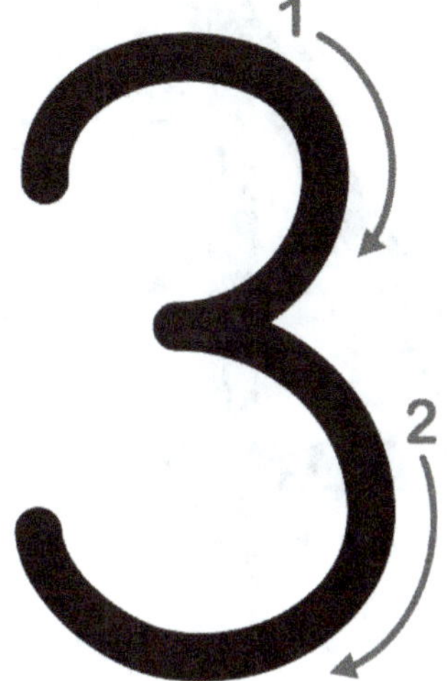

3 3 3 3
Three   Three

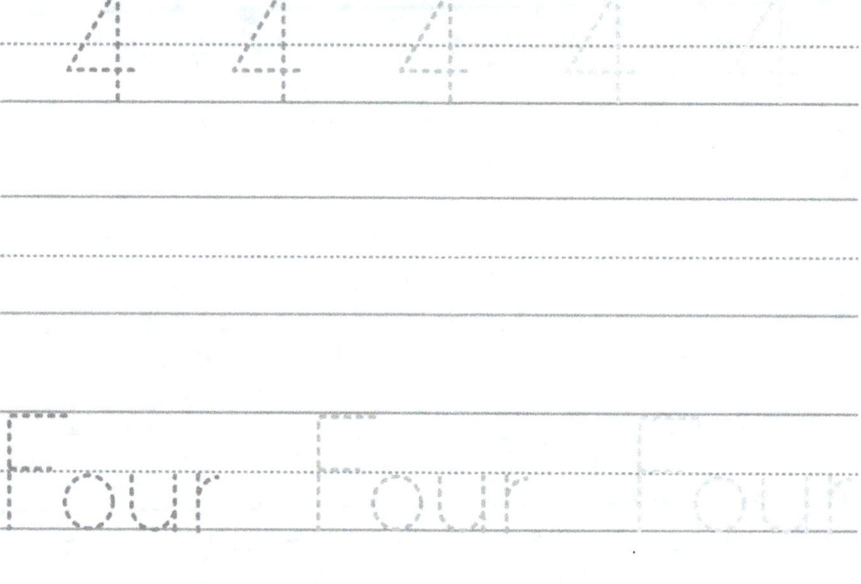

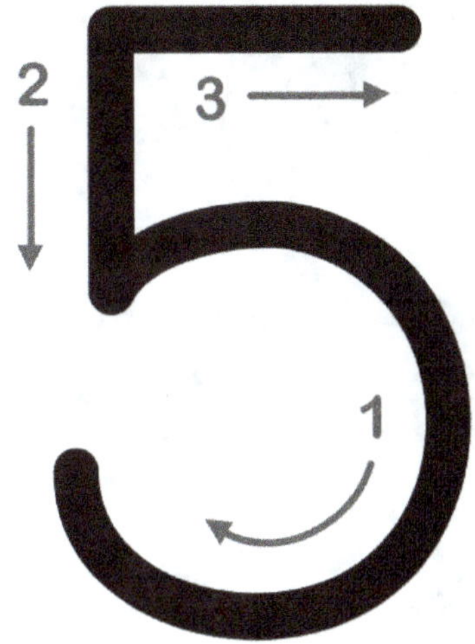

7
1
2
Seven Seven

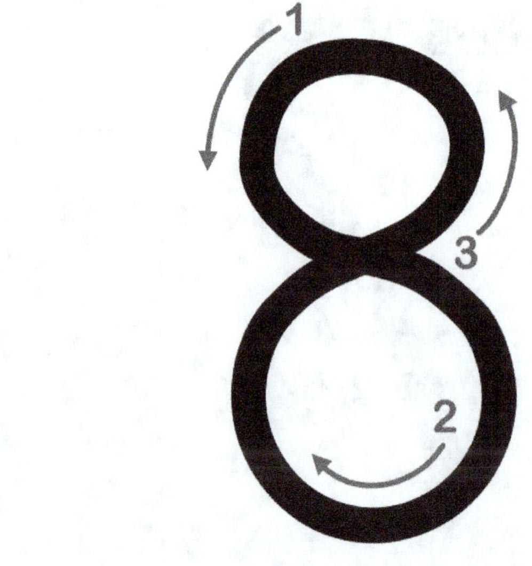

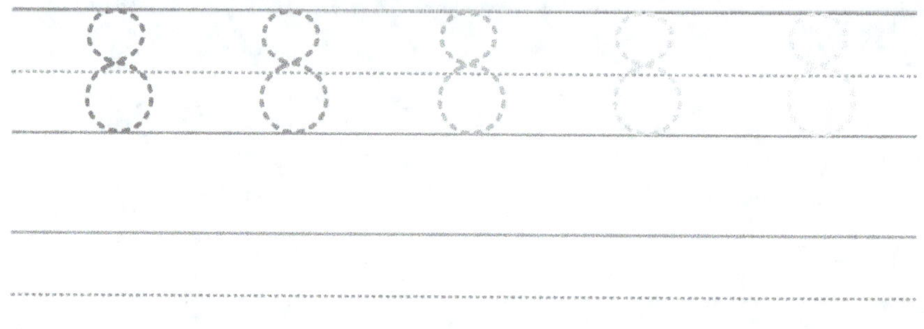

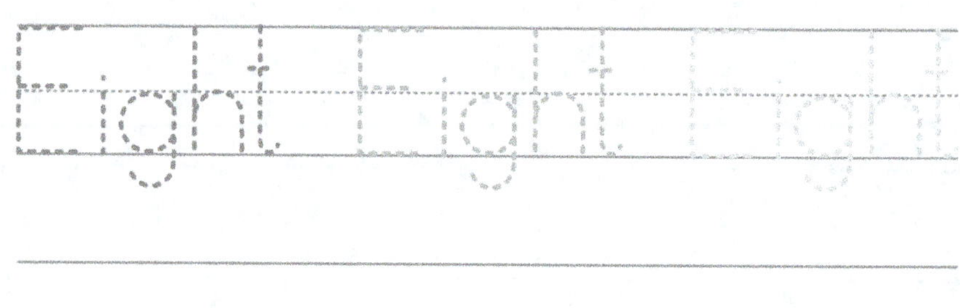
Eight Eight Eight

1
2
3
9 9 9 9 9
Nine Nine Nine

www.ingramcontent.com/pod-product-compliance
Lightning Source LLC
Chambersburg PA
CBHW082104130726
48003CB00009BA/3055